Radical Sports

BMX BIKING

Uncle Buck

Heinemann
LIBRARY

www.heinemann/library.co.uk
Visit our website to find out more information about Heinemann Library books.

To order:
☎ Phone 44 (0) 1865 888066
🖹 Send a fax to 44 (0) 1865 314091
🖥 Visit the Heinemann Library Bookshop at www.heinemann/library.co.uk to browse our catalogue and order online.

First published in Great Britain by Heinemann Library,
Halley Court, Jordan Hill, Oxford OX2 8EJ,
a division of Reed Educational and Professional Publishing Ltd.
Heinemann is a registered trademark of Reed Educational & Professional Publishing Limited.

OXFORD   MELBOURNE   AUCKLAND
JOHANNESBURG   BLANTYRE   GABORONE
IBADAN   PORTSMOUTH NH (USA)   CHICAGO

Designed by Celia Floyd
Originated by Universal
Printed in Hong Kong by Wing King Tong

ISBN 0 431 03695 0
06 05 04 03 02
10 9 8 7 6 5 4 3 2 1

British Library Cataloguing in Publication Data

Buck, Uncle
  BMX biking. – (Radical sports)
  1. Bicycle motocross – Juvenile literature
  I. Title
  796.6

Acknowledgements

The Publishers would like to thank the following for permission to reproduce photographs: All photos by Neill Phillips except pp4, 29b Corbis and pp6, 7, 29a Rich More.

Cover photograph reproduced with permission of Neill Phillips.

Our thanks to Phil Townsend of the British Cycling Federation and to Jane Bingham for their help in the preparation of this book.

Every effort has been made to contact copyright holders of any material reproduced in this book. Any omissions will be rectified in subsequent printings if notice is given to the Publisher.

This book aims to cover all the essential techniques of this radical sport but it is important when learning a new sport to get expert tuition and to follow any manufacturers' instructions.

CONTENTS

INTRODUCTION

A short history

BMX stands for bicycle motocross. The sport of BMX has its roots in Southern California in the early 1970s, where kids wanted to be like their motocross heroes, jumping and racing their cycles the way their heroes did with their motorbikes. As motorbikes were too heavy for small kids to handle, the BMX bike was invented.

During the 1970s a range of BMX bikes were developed by companies such as DG and Schwinn, (makers of the famous Stingray), Redline, Mongoose and GT. The early bikes were heavy and robust, but later on frames were made from **chromoly** and aluminium, making the bikes lighter and stronger.

One of the first BMX races was held in a supermarket car park in California. Soon after dirt tracks were built and the sport became organized, with racing all over the USA. By the early 1980s BMX racing had spread to Europe, and then on to the rest of the world. The first World Championship of BMX Racing was held in Dayton, Ohio in 1982.

This is an early race from the 1970s.

Riding a BMX is the perfect way to stay healthy and have fun.

Races and competitions

Over the next ten to fifteen years, different styles of BMX riding developed. Racing, where riders ride around a track with jumps and turns, is where BMX riding began as a sport. The other type of riding is BMX freestyle, where riders perfect tricks and skills similar to skateboarding. Freestyle is the general term used for **dirt**, **street**, **vert** and **flatland**. These four types of BMX allow riders to pull off specific tricks and ride in a more unstructured and non-competitive way.

Why ride BMX?

A BMX bike is the perfect way for anyone to start riding a bike. It provides healthy exercise while having the joy and freedom of riding. The fun of riding a BMX bike lies in the fact that because they are normally lighter and stronger than other bikes, it is easier to jump, race and put the bike where you want it to go. Riding a BMX is a complete lifestyle of expression and fun – once hooked, you'll never want to give it up.

WHAT IS BMX?

There are many different types of BMX riding and bikes. You should know about each of them so that you know what you can get out of the sport.

BMX racing

BMX racing takes place on a prepared track with jumps and banked turns or corners called **berms**. The aim is to get around the track as fast as possible. A race consists of up to eight riders racing a number of laps.

BMX freestyle

Dirt jumping is where riders ride on prepared dirt jumps which are normally bigger than on race tracks. This allows the riders to get 'big air' (rise up a long way above the ground) to pull off tricks in mid-air.

Street riding is just that, riding with your friends or alone around the streets pulling and trying tricks. Riders use steps, rails and ledges to **grind** (you grind with **stunt pegs** on your wheels along a metal bar or edge of a ramp). Street riding can also be practised at a skatepark or on a specially designed street course that has different types of ramps.

Getting big air on a freestyle dirt jump.

US BMX star, Dave Mirra, vert riding on a halfpipe.

Vert riding (also known as ramp riding) is done on a full skateboard-style halfpipe. A halfpipe is a 'U'-shaped wooden ramp with a flat section at the bottom and a platform at either end. Riders pull tricks in mid-air and get 'big air' out of the top of the halfpipe.

Flatland is where riders do all of their stunts and tricks on the ground, such as concrete or tarmac.

Getting advice

The best place to begin is your local club or track where you can get basic coaching and tips to get you started. Most BMX clubs have weekly sessions that you can attend or specific 'starter days' for new riders. They may also organize coaching sessions or rider clinics at their tracks during the year. Local bike shops may have details of where the nearest BMX track is located. Never be afraid to ask other more experienced riders for information when you are at the track. Major bike companies with Elite or Pro riders also run their own rider clinics at tracks and do tours around the country. Finally, your national BMX governing body will also give you details on where your nearest BMX club is located.

THE RIGHT BMX BIKE FOR YOU

Bike size is very important. BMX bikes come with standard 20 inch wheels but the bike frame can range in size. A good bike shop will advise on sizes (see chart).

Height	Frame Size
4' and under	mini
4'–4'10"	junior
4'10"–5'8"	pro
5'8"–6'3"	XL
6'3" and up	XXL

Make sure you feel comfortable on the bike. You should be able to sit on the saddle with your feet touching the floor. You should not have to stretch too far to hold onto the handlebars. If your knees are hitting the handlebars when you ride then the bike is too small.

TOP TIP

🚲 Getting the right size bike is critical. Don't get a bike that is too big for you, or you won't be able to have full control over it. Also do not just go for the bike with the best colour or stickers. Choose your bike wisely.

Handlebars

The handlebars need to be the right width and height to help you control your bike. Also the bars need to be in line with the forks – too far back or forward can affect the handling of the bike.

Forks

The forks are made from the same metal as the frame and you will need a number plate when racing.

Frame size guideline

When considering buying a bike you will also need to decide what kind of BMX biking you want to do. There are both specific bikes for the different disciplines and also models that allow you to do everything.

A race bike will be lightweight to enable the rider to race round the track faster. It will also have different tyres to allow a better grip. A **dirt** bike will be heavier than a race bike as it has to be much stronger for jumping, but it can be used for racing too. **Freestyle** bikes are also heavier and stronger. They have **stunt pegs** fitted to the axles of the wheels. These allow you to **grind** and are there to stand on while performing tricks.

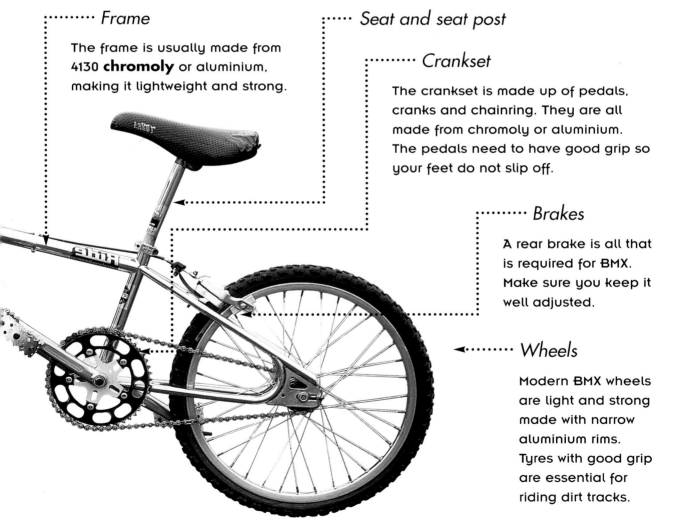

Frame

The frame is usually made from 4130 **chromoly** or aluminium, making it lightweight and strong.

Seat and seat post

Crankset

The crankset is made up of pedals, cranks and chainring. They are all made from chromoly or aluminium. The pedals need to have good grip so your feet do not slip off.

Brakes

A rear brake is all that is required for BMX. Make sure you keep it well adjusted.

Wheels

Modern BMX wheels are light and strong made with narrow aluminium rims. Tyres with good grip are essential for riding dirt tracks.

WHAT ELSE DO YOU NEED?

Basic equipment

Most BMX clubs have helmets and gloves which they hire out to riders. Second-hand protective equipment can often be bought at races for a bargain price, but make sure an expert checks it out first.

Clothing

For racing, the minimum clothing you will need is a long sleeve jersey or sweat top and long trousers or jeans to protect your arms and legs if you fall. A BMX race shirt is lightweight and vented to keep you cool and also offers protection while riding.

Gloves

A good, strong pair of leather gloves save your hands from falls and give good grip when riding. They also help prevent nasty calluses.

BMX helmet

A good helmet is vital to do any form of BMX riding. For **dirt** style riding, you will only need a basic dirt or skateboard style helmet. For **freestyle** or racing you will need a full face helmet for total protection. Your helmet size is critical as helmets need to be snug and are dangerous if too big.

Pad set for your bike

You will also need a pad set for your bike to cover stem, bars and top tube of frame. These pads will prevent you from hitting yourself (normally your knee) on these parts of the bike while riding.

Elbow and knee pads

Another part of your kit that will save injury and make you feel safer when riding.

Shoes

It is best to wear soft-soled skateboard type shoes or trainers to gain a good grip on the pedals. More experienced racers are starting to use clip-in pedals with shoes to give them faster acceleration and greater speed.

CHECKS AND PREPARATION

Checking your bike

You need to make sure your bike is safe and running correctly to achieve the best results. Check your chain is not slack, your wheels are not loose, you have enough air in your tyres and your brakes work. Also make sure your headset and handlebar stem are not loose.

Make sure that you check tyre pressure (left) and that your chain is not loose (above).

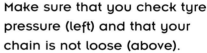

SAFETY FIRST

🚲 For safety always check your bike before going out to ride. Cover all the basic areas, such as tyres, wheels, brakes, cranks and handlebar stem.

At the track

You can learn a lot from experienced riders and if you are at the race track you can watch how they take the jumps, **berms** and lines around the track. Even top riders watch others if they are having a problem with a certain part of the track. If you can, walk the track to get a close look at the layout of the jumps and berms. Talk to the other riders to get tips. There are always organized practice sessions at BMX tracks to get yourself acquainted with the track.

Keeping fit and healthy

Before going out to ride it is advisable to do some warming up exercises on your hamstrings, calves, back and upper body. This will help you warm your muscles and reduce risk of straining. After a riding session you can cool down with a light gentle ride and some light stretching to save stiffness and muscle strain.

Hamstring stretch ·····························➤

Have one leg straight and the other bent. You should feel a stretch along the back of your straight leg. Hold for 10 seconds. Repeat six times for each leg.

Quadricep stretch ·····························

Standing on one leg, pull the other up behind you. Hold this position for 10 seconds and then do the other leg.

··········· *Upper body stretch*

Put hand under elbow and push arm back across chest and over shoulder. Repeat on other arm.

Nutrition

Eating the right food before riding or racing is very important. Do not eat a heavy meal just before you go out to ride your bike. Eat something light like cereal, bread or toast and fruit. While out riding you should eat little but often – fruit or energy bars are ideal. Also drink plenty of fluids while riding – water is normally best. All these items are light and can be easily packed in a small rucksack when going to the track.

MANUALS AND WHEELIES

Now you are ready to ride your BMX bike. Riding a BMX bike is really like riding any other bike apart from the fact that you will be able to have more control and find it easier to ride than heavier, larger-wheeled bikes. Most of all it will be lots more fun!

Wheelies and manuals

The first tricks you should learn are **wheelies** and **manuals**. They are similar in that they both involve the front wheel leaving the ground while riding.

Popping a wheelie takes a bit of practice. Try the move very slowly at first and on a flat surface away from the track.

1. Lean your body back.

2. Pull up the front with the handlebars.

3. At the same time keep pedalling and riding along.

1. Get your body in the right position and leaning back.

2. Lift the front wheel.

Being able to manual is very useful when riding any form of BMX, whether racing or **freestyling**. It allows you to get through jumps on a race track, such as **speed jumps**, **triples** or **whoops**, smoothly and fast without pedalling.

Timing and co-ordination during this move is crucial. This can take a long time to perfect so be patient. Practice makes perfect.

3. Let the bike glide over the jump while still moving along.

SAFETY FIRST

🚲 Remember to always put on all of your protective equipment before starting to ride, even if it is hot.

BUNNY HOPS AND JUMPS

Once you have practised **manuals** and **wheelies**, you are ready to learn how to do **bunny hops** and how to clear jumps. There are many different jumps you could face while riding including **table-tops**, **speed jumps**, **triples**, **whoops** or doubles and a technical section on a BMX track called a **rhythm section**.

Bunny hops

1. Grip your feet on the pedals, by trying to curl your feet around the pedals to get the grip, either while stationary or moving along.

2. Bend your knees slightly.

3. Lift the bike with both your hands and feet in a bouncing movement.

SAFETY FIRST

🚲 Make sure you are wearing all your protective equipment while trying these basic riding moves and at any other time whether on the track or the street.

Jumping doubles

This will take some time depending on your ability, strength and age. Work up to this very slowly and only attempt it if fully confident. Try some practice runs to get the right speed for attempting the jump first, by just riding through the double jump. Too much speed will send you too high and too far and too little speed will cause you to hit the second jump. Pumping on the downside of the jump will give you more speed to take the next jump, or allow you to ride faster along the next section of track.

1. Get your speed up and use the first jump as your take off point. Lift your bike slightly as you hit the **lip** at the top of the first jump.

2. Aim for the downside of the next jump so that you can land smoothly.

3. Keep your bars straight and your pedals horizontal.

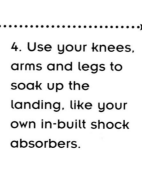

4. Use your knees, arms and legs to soak up the landing, like your own in-built shock absorbers.

TAKING A BERM

A **berm** is a banked sloped turn on a BMX track. They can be various sizes and angles. Riding a berm correctly can give you a good advantage in a race. It will give you more speed coming out of the berm to take jumps. It may also block another rider from behind or allow you to pass them.

Basic tactics

The route you take on the track is called the line. Practising the lines you take on a berm is crucial as sometimes just following another rider's line will not allow you to try a passing move to get into the lead. There are three basic tactics to riding a berm – high-low for passing, low-high to protect your position and **railing** (riding as fast as you can to gain maximum speed) the turn for speed.

High-low

1. Approach the berm high on the outside. This is called riding the high line.

2. Gather speed and rail around the berm high until you are near the middle or towards the exit of the berm.

3. Then you're ready to swoop down or pass the other rider to the inside.

Low-high

1. Stay low to middle of the track with your approach to the berm.

2. Ride up the berm.

3. Then ride round protecting your inside from other riders diving under you.

Railing

Approach the berm, railing as fast as you can, and ride the berm through a line from the middle to top. Gain as much speed as you can on your exit to attempt passing on the next **straight** or to give you better speed and momentum to take a jump.

Try to practise the different berm lines with a few friends at the track. Not only will it improve your riding, it will be loads of fun.

HOW TO START A RACE

The start is the most important part of a BMX race. If you get a bad start you will find it hard to fight your way through the pack. Most top riders work on their starts more than any other aspect of training.

The area on a BMX track where you start in a race has a gate that drops down. Most tracks have a light and sound sequence that triggers the gate. The lights are like a traffic light system with a voice activated command used internationally, saying "Ok riders, lets set 'em up… riders ready… watch the gate or lights". This command can also have a set of beeps going with the lights.

Getting ready to go

Before you start a race you will have to line up in your starting position against the gate and wait for it to drop. There are two basic methods of starting a race. For beginners there is the one-footed start, but the more popular method is the two-footed start.

Balance and push up against the gate waiting to start. Concentrate on the lights, voice command and beeps.

One-footed start

One foot should be on the start pad on the ground by your bike's back wheel and one on the pedal. As the gate goes down the rider throws his or her weight forward at the same time as putting the back foot on the pedal and pushing out of the gate and riding away.

Two-footed start

For a two-footed start, try to begin in a standing position with both feet on the pedals. This is made easier as the shape of the start hill will naturally push your bike into the gate, but a good tip is to sit down whilst arranging your feet on the pedals with your strongest or most comfortable foot forward. Sitting means that it will be easier to balance at first and you will not wobble as much. When you feel stable, stand up, straighten your arms and move your weight to the back of the bike, ready to push out of the gate when it goes down.

To get a snap is to get a good start out of the gate. A holeshot is where the rider holds the lead out of the gate and down to the first jump or to the bottom of the start hill at the beginning of the race.

When the gate drops, throw your body and bike forward and push out and peddle as fast as you can down the start hill.

SAFETY AND RULES

Getting signed up to race

When you get to the track, the first thing you need to do is find out where you can sign up to race. Usually it is inside a small building, trailer or maybe even a tent. Here you can sign up and become a member of a club. You will fill in a card with your age, race plate number, category (could be novice or expert) and date of birth. A club official will always be on hand to advise you. You will then be put in a race called a **moto** with other riders of your age and category.

You will start by having three motos. Just after practice the moto sheets will be posted and you can check to see what race you are in. Make a note of the race number and your three allocated gate positions. An official will call up the riders before their motos. Check the moto sheets after each qualifying round. You need to be on your bike, wearing your full protective equipment, at the back of the start hill or pre-staging area at least ten races before your race.

Keep safe. Wear all your safety gear while riding and follow the rules at races.

Safety and rules

BMX is a very exciting and extreme sport, but it can be dangerous if you do not follow some basic safety rules.

Do not ride when you are tired. Most accidents and crashes happen at the end of the day or session.

It is very important to obey the flags at all times.

On race days at the track there will be officials to help with the running of the race. The chief referee on the track will also have two or three marshals to help. They will have coloured flags; red, yellow and green. Red is to stop racing – only the senior referee has this flag. Yellow is to pause a race if a rider is down and a green flag allows the race to go ahead.

TOP TIP

🚲 For racing you will have to remove **stunt pegs**, chain guards, reflectors that stick out and kickstands.

SAFETY FIRST

🚲 Replace any worn or broken equipment on your bike before riding.

🚲 Always wear all the safety equipment at all times while riding.

🚲 Always choose a safe place to ride.

🚲 Watch out for other riders at the track or skatepark.

🚲 Always ride the correct way round the race track.

🚲 When racing, always have a full set of pads on your bike.

🚲 Take your time and do not attempt difficult jumps or tricks until you are ready.

🚲 Keep your riding area clean and tidy.

CARING FOR YOUR BIKE

Expert riders or other members of a BMX club can teach you how to care for your bike. The most important parts on your bike to check are what we call the running gear – the chain, wheels, **hubs**, cranks, chainrings (front), **freewheel (rear sprocket)** and tyres.

To help look after your bike you will need a basic tool kit with 10–15mm size spanners, allen keys of different sizes and a pump and puncture kit. You will need the spanners to tighten wheels and pedals, and allen keys to tighten stems, seat post clamps etc. Always use the right size tool for your bike, or you may damage it.

AF allen keys | tyre pressure guage | metric allen keys

multi-purpose spanner | plastic tyre lever | puncture repair kit

Oil your chain regularly, wiping off excess with a cloth, and check for wear. Your wheels should always spin straight. Check for loose or missing **spokes** and your hubs should spin freely. If your wheel rubs against your brake it is a sign that either your wheel alignment is out or your wheel is buckled. If it is not too bent it can be fixed with a spoke key, but it needs to be done at a bike shop or by someone who has experience with wheel building.

TOP TIP

🚲 Regular cleaning of your bike not only makes your bike look good, but is a good way to discover problems with your bike as well. There are special cleaners for bikes, but soap and warm water will do. Never jet wash or hose your bike unless absolutely necessary, as it can get into the moving parts and bearings.

The crankset

The cranks need to be able to spin freely and have no play. Check the nuts on the spindles as cranks have a tendency to work loose. Make sure the front chainring is not bent and that it does not have any teeth missing. Also check chainring bolts if you have them.

The rear brake

Keep your brakes adjusted properly and check the pads for wear. Do not let the pads rub on the tyre as that will wear them down.

The tyres

Check the freewheel for play, slippage, teeth missing and wear. It is vital that you run the correct tyre pressure as this can affect the handling and feel of the bike. Also check your tyres regularly for wear around the walls and tread. A tyre with no tread will puncture easily and give you no grip.

TAKING IT FURTHER

Most of the BMX governing bodies around the world host a Junior Development programme to encourage new young riders into the sport of BMX. Contact them to get more information (see page 31 for details).

There are some guidelines to follow if you want to progress in BMX racing. However, note that reaching step four (see page 27) is not going to happen overnight. As in all sports, you will need practice and training to become a competent rider. Take one step at a time and enjoy it.

12-year-old Liam Phillips is one of Britain's top riders.

Coaching for new riders is available at your local BMX club.

Guidelines to progression in BMX racing

1. BMX clubs are where you start. The Club Officials and more experienced riders will give you all the help and information to get you started. You can then sign up to Coaching and Rider clinics and Junior Development programmes.

2. Your club will run practice nights and Open Club Races that you can take part in.

3. Once you become more confident you can race at regional level and at National Series Events where you can receive a national or regional ranking at the end of the series. Most countries run regional races where a rider can enter at a beginner stage in a novice or intermediate class and work his or her way up to expert when they feel they have had enough experience. Many clubs also run the same structure.

4. Once you get to a level where you have a national ranking you may be invited by your national governing body to race at international events all over the world.

A new rider practising his starts and joining in the fun of a BMX race.

TOP TIP

🚲 Riders under the age of 16 need specific advice on training. Seek professional advice from a nationally recognised coach.

THE INTERNATIONAL SCENE

BMX has grown over the years, becoming popular all over the world. Each year the UCI (Union Cycliste Internationale) World Championships are held in various countries around the world. The UCI is the governing body of international BMX. Most continents, such as Europe, South America and North America, also hold their own championships.

In the USA the sport is massive with two National Organizations, the ABA and the NBL, who both run their own National Series. The ABA hold the 'Grands' every year, which is the biggest BMX race in the world, attended by thousands of riders.

BMX is also big in Australia. Wade Bootes and Warwick Stevenson are two of the top Pros in the world, with Stevenson being the 2001 ABA No.1 Pro in the USA. Australia also have one of the top female BMX racers in the world with Natarsha Williams, who was World Champion in Elite Woman in 2000 and is now a top Pro Women rider in the USA.

Natarsha Williams of Australia, one of the top female riders in the world.

BMX is popular in Britain and has been an organized sport with a governing body since the early 1980s. There are currently around 40 affiliated BMX clubs in Britain. They host the BCF BMX National Series at various tracks around the country and also the British BMX Championships. In the 1980s the Kelloggs BMX series was shown on TV in the UK and resulted in getting more people into BMX in the UK than at any other time. Great Britain's Dale Holmes is one of the top riders in the world. He was the UCI Elite Mens World Champion in 1996 and 2001 and holds nine World Championship medals.

Great Britain's Dale Holmes, UCI World Champion in 1996 and 2001.

As well as BMX races, there are also international competitions for **vert**, **street** and **dirt** riding. The best ones include the EXPN X Games, Gravity Games, Urban Games and World Extreme Games. These events have been shown on TV, bringing BMX to a worldwide audience, making the likes of Dave Mirra and Ryan Nyquist both from the USA, worldwide sports stars.

Dave Mirra is one of the most famous and most successful freestylers in the world.

GLOSSARY

berm a banked turn or corner on a BMX track

bunny hop lifting your bike up by gripping the pedals with your feet

chromaly lightweight aircraft metal tubing

dirt where riders perform jump variations over specially constructed dirt jumps

flatland where riders perform tricks on the ground

freestyle all styles of trick riding

freewheel or **rear sprocket** a small cog on the rear wheel that is driven by the chain

grind to use your stunt pegs to slide on the top edge of a ramp or metal rail

high line riding at the top or outside of the berm

hub centre of the wheel

lip the take off point of a jump

manual doing a wheelie without pedalling

moto a BMX race. One of three qualifying races.

pumping when a rider has to use a pumping motion to lift and push down on or off a jump to gain more speed. It is also a term used when a rider has to ride through a rhythm section pumping his bike and shifting his body weight back and forth to get through it, pulling and pushing the bike up and down.

rail to ride a berm as fast as you can to get maximum speed on the exit

rhythm section a group of jumps placed close together on a track to make a rider pump, manual or jump smoothly through it

speed jump single rounded jump on the track that you ride over

speed wheelie picking up or lifting your front wheel before a jump

spokes thin circular metal rods that are attached to the rim and hub of the wheel

straight a section of track that has jumps on it

street where riders ride on constructed courses with various wooden jumps, rails and quarterpipes representing normal street obstacles; also means to ride on the street

stunt pegs these are attached to wheel axles to allow grinding and balancing

swoop to pass another rider on a berm

table-top a jump on a track with a flat top; a trick in the air getting the bike horizontal

triples speed jumps set out in three parts

vert halfpipe riding

wheelie lifting your front wheel while riding along pedalling

whoops (also known as doubles) set of two speed jumps on a track that you can ride through or jump

USEFUL ADDRESSES

UK

British Cycling
National Cycling Centre
Stuart Street
Manchester
M11 4DQ
Tel: 0161 230 2301
Email: info@britishcycling.org.uk

SCU (Scottish Cyclists' Union)
The Velodrome
London Road
Edinburgh
EH7 6AD
Tel: 0131 652 0187
Email: scottish.cycling@btinternet.com

World

UCI (Union Cycliste Internationale)
37 Route de Chavannes
Case Postale 1000
Lausanne 23
Switzerland
Tel: (+41) 21 622 0580
Email: admin@uci.ch

Australia

BMX Australia
Bicycle Motocross Inc.
Ground Floor 120 Jolimont Road
Jolimont 3002

P.O Box 334 East Melbourne
Victoria 8002
Tel: 61 3 96542790
Email: bmxa@ocean.com.au

FURTHER READING

Books

BMX Bikes (Cruisin), Karol Carstensen and Jamie Mosberg, Capstone Press

Bicycle Stunt Riding, Jason Glaser, Capstone Press

BMX Racing (Action Sports), Bill Gutman and Gork, Capstone Press

Learning How – BMX Biking, Sue Boulais, Bancroft Sage Publishing

BMX Bicycles, Barbara Knox, Capstone Press

Magazines

BMX Plus, Hi-Torque Publications

Ride, 4130 Publishing

Transworld BMX, Time 4 Media

Websites

www.bcf.uk.com
British Cycling governing body

www.uci.ch
UCI, the world governing body of cycle sport

www.bmxaustralia.com.au
BMX Australia

www.bmxracing-dirt.com
UK website of Uncle Buck

All the Internet addresses (URLs) given in this book were valid at the time of going to press. However, due to the dynamic nature of the Internet, some addresses may have changed, or sites may have ceased to exist since publication. While the author and publishers regret any inconvenience this may cause readers, no responsibility for any such changes can be accepted by either the author or the publishers.

INDEX

Titles in the *Radical Sports* series include:

Hardback   0 431 03695 0

Hardback   0 431 03690 X

Hardback   0 431 03692 6

Hardback   0 431 03691 8

Hardback   0 431 03694 2

Hardback   0 431 03693 4

Find out about the other titles in this series on our website www.heinemann.co.uk/library